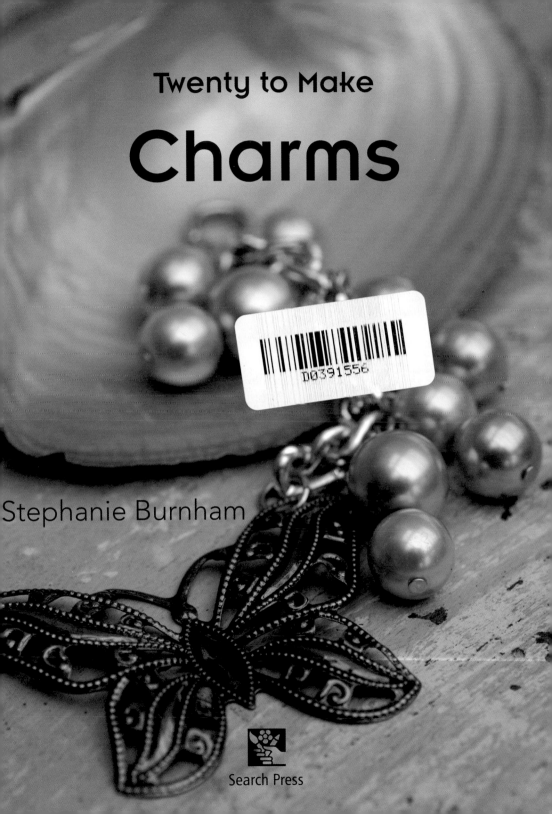

Twenty to Make

Charms

Stephanie Burnham

Search Press

First published in Great Britain 2007

Search Press Limited
Wellwood, North Farm Road,
Tunbridge Wells, Kent TN2 3DR

Reprinted 2009

Text copyright © Stephanie Burnham 2007

Photographs by Debbie Patterson at
Search Press Studios and on location

Photographs and design copyright
© Search Press Ltd. 2007

ISBN: 978-1-84448-275-7

The Publishers and author can accept no
responsibility for any consequences arising from
the information, advice or instructions given in
this publication.

Suppliers
If you have difficulty in obtaining any of the
materials and equipment mentioned in this book,
then please visit the Search Press website for
details of suppliers: www.searchpress.com

Printed in Malaysia

Dedication
For my mum, always the height of
fashion, style and innovative ideas;
all my creative talents are from you,
love you lots. x

Bead sizes	
4mm $=$ $^3/_{16}$in	
6mm $=$ $^1/_4$in	
8mm $=$ $^5/_{16}$in	

Contents

Introduction

I was thrilled when first asked to design twenty charms for a book. All my other books have been based around beadweaving, so to enter the world of fashion, which I love, is wonderful.

I wanted to incorporate as many different colours and textures as possible in the charms. Within the range are both classic and funky designs, with something for all ages.

Fashion jewellery is surprisingly easy to make: all that is needed is a good set of pliers and some interesting and diverse beads, pendants and fashion jewellery components. After making several projects from this book you will find yourself hunting around flea markets and second-hand shops for interesting pieces to add to your charms.

One of the loveliest things about creating charms is that you can admire them every day, either on a handbag, attached to a set of keys, or just hanging on a hook around the home as decoration. The choices are endless.

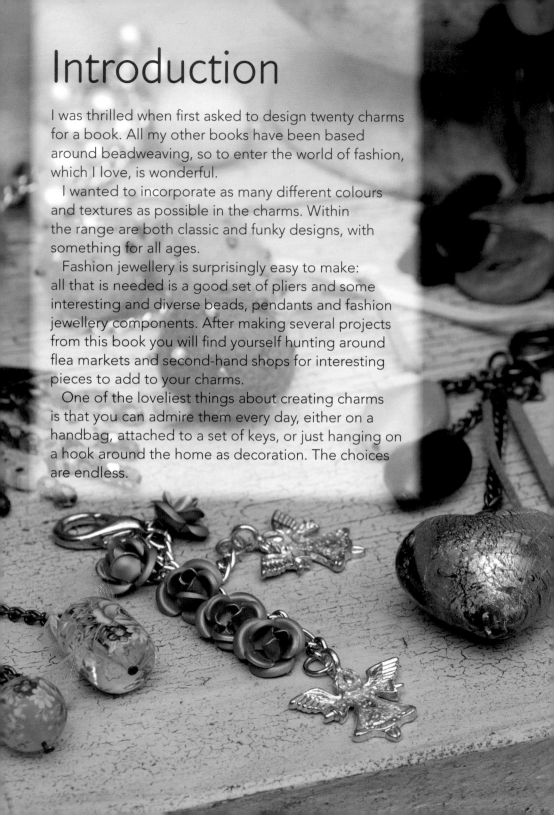

Heart Happening

Materials:

1 x glass heart bead
2 x glass beads
Suede ribbon
Medium craft chain
8 x jump rings
5 x pink seed beads
2 x flat leather crimps
3 x headpins
Keyring fob

Tools:

Cutting pliers
Round-nosed pliers
Flat-nosed pliers

Instructions:

1 Wire the three glass beads with headpins, creating a loop at the top of each bead and adding a pink seed bead at either end of the rectangular glass bead and one pink seed bead below and one above the heart bead.

2 Attach three differing lengths of chain to the keyring fob using jump rings. Attach the three glass beads to the bottom of the three lengths of chain, again using jump rings.

3 Cut two lengths of suede ribbon and attach a flat leather crimp to one end of each using flat-nosed pliers.

4 Using jump rings, attach the suede ribbons to the keyring fob. You can then cut the bottom end of the ribbon at an angle to give a neat finish.

Spring Heart

A copper-coloured chain, clasp and jump rings are used to set off green beads and suede ribbons, creating a lush, spring-like feel to this charm.

Pastel Pearls

Materials:

A selection of faux pearl beads

4 x large wrapped beads

4 x 4mm fire-polished crystals

Medium copper-coloured craft chain

14 x headpins

1 x copper-coloured jump ring

Large copper-coloured lobster clasp

Tools:

Cutting pliers

Round-nosed pliers

Instructions:

1 Wire a selection of pearl beads on to headpins, creating a loop at the top of each set of beads.

2 Do the same with the four wrapped beads using a 4mm fire-polished crystal at the base of each bead.

3 Cut a section of chain to the required length and attach it to the large lobster clasp using a jump ring.

4 Finally, carefully open up each loop at the top of each set of beads and attach to the chain one by one.

Pretty in Pearls

A silver-coloured chain is teamed with beads in cool blue and pink to make a sumptuous but subtle charm that looks great attached to a purse.

Eastern Flowers

Materials:

1 x large accent bead
2 x medium accent beads
Suede ribbon
Organza ribbon
Medium silver-coloured
    craft chain
8 silver-coloured
    jump rings
3 x headpins
2 x silver-coloured flat
    leather crimps
1 x large silver-coloured
    lobster clasp

Tools:

Cutting pliers
Round-nosed pliers
Flat-nosed pliers

Instructions:

1 Using headpins, wire the three accent beads, creating a loop at the top of each bead.

2 Attach three varying lengths of chain to the large lobster clasp with jump rings.

3 Attach the three glass beads to the bottom ends of the chain, again with jump rings.

4 Cut two lengths of suede ribbon and attach a flat leather crimp to one end of each using flat-nosed pliers.

5 Attach the two lengths of suede to the large lobster clasp with jump rings. The bottom ends of the suede can then be cut at an angle to give a nice finish.

6 Finally, cut three pieces of ribbon about 5cm (2in) long, thread a ribbon through each jump ring attaching an accent bead and tie a double knot. The ribbon can then be cut off at an angle to the required length.

Oriental Garden

*These flower-painted accent beads give an oriental
feel to a charm. Instead of the blue, try a pink and
green theme. The little wisps of organza ribbon
make the prettiest finishing touch.*

Fairytale Butterfly

Materials:

A selection of faux pearls

Large butterfly charm

Medium copper-coloured craft chain

10 x copper-coloured jump rings

9 x headpins

Large copper-coloured lobster clasp

Tools:

Cutting pliers

Round-nosed pliers

Instructions:

1 Wire a selection of pearl beads on to headpins, creating a loop at the top of each set of beads.

2 Cut a piece of chain the required length and attach it to the large lobster clasp using a jump ring.

3 Using round-nosed pliers, open up a jump ring, slip a wired pearl bead on to it, then slip the jump ring on to the central chain and close it.

4 Continue adding pearls in the same manner until the charm is complete.

5 Attach the butterfly charm to the end of the chain using a jump ring.

Pearly Butterfly

Change from the warm, gold and bronze tones of the charm opposite to make this pretty variation using pastel-coloured pearls with silver and a more delicate butterfly.

Gardener's Delight

Materials:

5 x themed charms

Medium gold-coloured
  craft chain

8 x gold-coloured
  jump rings

Large gold-coloured
  lobster clasp

Tools:

Cutting pliers

Round-nosed pliers

Instructions:

1 Cut three pieces of chain of varying lengths.

2 Attach all three lengths to the lobster clasp
with jump rings.

3 Using a jump ring, attach a charm to the
base of all three chain lengths.

4 Add the last two charms to the two
longer lengths of chain about
one-third of the way up the
chain lengths.

Summer Fun

*Beaded flip-flops complete this sizzling charm,
which would make a lovely gift for someone with a
summer birthday.*

Hippy Chick

Materials:

9 x mother of pearl dyed shapes

11 x gold-coloured jump rings

2 x headpins

2 x feature beads

4 x seed beads

Large gold-coloured lobster clasp

Tools:

Cutting pliers

Round-nosed pliers

Instructions:

1 Take a single jump ring, open it up using round-nosed pliers, thread on a round and a square shape and close the jump ring.

2 Repeat until you have four shapes joined together.

3 Make a second chain link, this time with five shapes.

4 Attach the chain with five links to the large lobster clasp, then attach the chain with four shapes to the jump ring of the chain with five links.

5 Wire the two feature beads on to headpins, placing a seed bead at the top and bottom of each larger bead.

6 Attach each bead to the bottom end of a chain link using a jump ring.

Pretty in Pink

This version of the charm looks great with jeans, and the luscious feature beads add a touch of class.

Bubble Gum

Materials:

3 x large beaded beads
6 x small faux pearls
2 x medium faux pearls
Large silver-coloured craft chain
6 x headpins
9 x silver-coloured jump rings
Silver-coloured keyring fob

Tools:

Cutting pliers
Round-nosed pliers

Instructions:

1 Wire the large beaded beads on to headpins, placing a small pearl bead at the top and bottom of each bead, and creating a loop at the top of each set of beads. Here, the smaller beaded bead did not need a pearl at the top; just use your own judgment when choosing beads.

2 Cut three pieces of craft chain of varying lengths and attach them to the keyring fob with jump rings.

3 Attach the three beaded beads to the base of each chain using jump rings, placing the largest bead on to the longest length of chain.

4 Wire the remaining pearls on to headpins and attach them to the chain as you wish.

Red-Hot

This red and gold version of the charm makes a really dazzling decoration for a plain bag.

Celebration Hearts

Materials:

1 large shell heart

2 x silver-coloured hearts

3 x glass feature beads

Large silver-coloured craft chain

3 x headpins

9 x jump rings

Keyring fob

Tools:

Cutting pliers

Round-nosed pliers

Instructions:

1 Wire all three feature beads with headpins, creating a loop at the top of each bead.

2 Cut three varying lengths of chain and attach to the keyring fob with jump rings.

3 Attach the large heart to the longest length of chain, and the two slightly smaller hearts to the other two chain ends, all with jump rings.

4 Finally position all three feature beads onto the chain lengths with jump rings.

Hearts and Gold

Glitzy gold and cream-coloured hearts make this charm the perfect accessory for a leather bag.

Traveller's Tale

Materials:

2 x large copper-coloured beads
3 x medium copper-coloured beads
10 x heart-shaped copper-
    coloured spacer beads
5 x headpins
Large copper-coloured craft chain
6 x jump rings
Large copper-coloured lobster clasp

Tools:

Cutting pliers
Round-nosed pliers

Instructions:

1 Cut three pieces of craft chain of varying lengths and attach them to the large lobster clasp using one large jump ring.

2 Wire up the two large and three medium metal beads, placing one spacer bead at the top and bottom of each.

3 Attach the two larger and one medium wired-up beads to the base of each chain length.

4 Attach one of the two remaining medium beads directly to the lobster clasp with a jump ring.

5 Attach the second half-way up the longest length of chain, again using a jump ring.

Silver Charmer

This charm looks great against dark clothes or bags,
and could even be used to brighten a dark corner
of your house.

Venetian Splendour

Materials:
2 x large glass
   feature beads

3 x medium glass
   feature beads

1 x 8mm bicone crystal

6 x headpins

Large silver-coloured
   lobster clasp

Tools:
Cutting pliers

Round-nosed pliers

Instructions:
1 Cut the head from a
headpin, thread the piece
of wire through one of the
glass feature beads and
create a loop at each end of
the bead.

2 Repeat in the same
manner until all five beads
have two loops each.

3 Take one of the large
beads, carefully open up
one of the loops and slip the
lobster clasp on to the loop.
Close the loop again.

4 Open the loop at the
other end and slip on the
second big bead, closing
the loop afterwards.

5 Repeat until all five beads
are joined together using
the links created.

6 To finish, wire the crystal
bead up and fix to the
loop of the last feature
bead added.

Amber Elegance

This alternative version of the charm replaces cool pink with amber tones to create a precious-looking golden glow.

First Love

Materials:

Glass heart feature bead
5 x faux pearls
Medium silver-coloured
  craft chain
Jump ring
4 x headpins
Large silver-coloured
  lobster clasp

Tools:

Cutting pliers
Round-nosed pliers

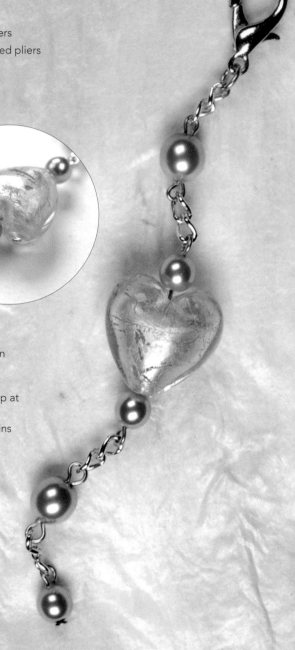

Instructions:

1 Remove the head from a headpin, then thread on one pearl, a glass heart and a pearl.

2 Using round-nosed pliers, create a loop at each end of the beads.

3 Wire up two other pearls using headpins and make loops at both ends of these two beads.

4 Cut four sections of chain containing only two links per section.

5 Using a jump ring, attach the first two links to the lobster clasp, then open up one of the loops on the single pearls and thread it through the second link from the clasp.
Close it again with round-nosed pliers.

6 Continue to open and close links as you work towards the base of the charm.

7 To finish, wire the final pearl onto a headpin and attach to the last link of the chain.

Golden Heart
*This sumptuous golden version of the charm makes a
beautiful gift for a loved one.*

Posh Pom-Poms

Materials:

3 x large beaded felt balls

Medium gold-coloured craft chain

Jump ring

3 x headpins

Gold-coloured keyring fob

Suede ribbon in two colours

4 x flower sequins

Tools:

Cutting pliers

Round-nosed pliers

Instructions:

1 Take two of the felt balls and wire them on to headpins, adding a flower sequin at each end. Create a loop at the top of each bead.

2 Cut two 15cm (6in) lengths of suede ribbon. Place the two pieces together and thread them through the loop on the keyring fob. Tie the lengths together using a single knot underneath the fixing point of the keyring fob.

3 Take the third felt ball and thread it on to one of the lengths of suede. Cut the suede to the length you require then make a knot below the felt ball to secure it.

4 Trim the remaining lengths of suede to the desired length, cutting at an angle for a neat finish.

5 Cut a length of chain, attach it to the keyring fob with a jump ring, and then attach the two wired beads to the chain as desired.

Moody Blues
Blue and purple felt balls teamed with silver add a touch of subtlety to a chunky charm.

Dotty Daydream

Materials:

4 x glass feature beads

2 x 8mm round beads

50cm (19¾in) rat
tail cord

Suede ribbon

2 x flat leather crimps

Jump ring

Large gold-coloured
lobster clasp

Tools:

Cutting pliers

Round-nosed pliers

Instructions:

1 Cut two lengths of suede ribbon and attach flat leather crimps
to one end of each.

2 Pass one end of the rat tail cord through the fixing point on the lobster
clasp. When you reach the halfway point in the cord, place the two side by
side and make a single knot underneath the fixing point of the clasp.

3 Just before you finally tighten the knot, open a jump ring and place the
two suede ribbon pieces on to the ring, slip the open ring into the knot
then close the ring as usual. This traps the suede nicely.

4 To add the beads, simply make a single knot on one of the cord ends
just below the main knot, slip the glass bead on to the cord then make a
second knot just below the bead.

5 Continue adding beads and knotting until all the beads are added.
Finally, cut the suede off to whatever length you wish, using an angled cut.

Blue Yonder

Turquoise, blue and pink with weird and wonderful bumpy beads make this charm a dotty delight.

Girls' Best Friends

Materials:

2 x glass beads

1 x handbag and
  2 x shoe charms

Medium silver-coloured
  craft chain

7 x jump rings

2 x headpins

Large silver-coloured
  lobster clasp

Tools:

Cutting pliers

Round-nosed pliers

Instructions:

1 Wire the two glass beads on to headpins, creating a loop at the top of each bead.

2 Cut two lengths of chain at varying lengths, and then attach both to the large lobster clasp using a jump ring.

3 Attach the handbag to the longer length of chain, then one of the shoes to the shorter length, using jump rings.

4 Place the second shoe just above the first one so they sit almost as a pair.

5 Finally, place the two glass beads further up the lengths of chain, using jump rings.

New Shoes

Two lengths of suede ribbon attached to flat leather crimps were added to the alternate colourway instead of feature beads to ring the changes.

Guardian Angels

Materials:

2 x gold-coloured
  angel charms

5 x gold rose beads

Medium gold-coloured
  craft chain

3 x jump rings

5 x headpins

Gold-coloured
  lobster clasp

Tools:

Cutting pliers
Round-nosed pliers

Instructions:

1 Take all five gold rose beads and wire them on to separate headpins, forming a loop at the top of each bead.

2 Cut two lengths of craft chain, one shorter than the other and attach both to the large lobster clasp using a jump ring.

3 Attach an angel charm to the base of each chain with a jump ring.

4 Bend the headpins in the gold roses to one side so that the roses will lay nicely on the charm. Finally, secure the roses to the chain wherever you wish.

Angels and Crystals

The alternate colourway has been made using 6mm fire-polished crystals instead of gold roses. Together with the glittery angels they give this charm a frosty appeal, ideal for a winter gift.

Button Chic

Materials:

A selection of buttons

Organza ribbon

Large silver-coloured
   lobster clasp

Tools:

Scissors

Collapsible eye needle

Instructions:

1 Pass one end of the ribbon
through the fixing point on
the large lobster clasp. Hold
both sides of the ribbon
together and tie in a single
knot just underneath the
fixing point.

2 Thread the collapsible
eye needle on to one end of
the organza, then thread the
buttons on to the ribbon one
by one. There need to be two
sets of three buttons on each
piece of ribbon, finished with
a knot at the base of each.

All Buttoned Up

*The red and green colourway with a copper-coloured clasp creates a
fresh-looking charm that looks great with natural materials.*

Bronze Bloom

Materials:

Large bronze flower

Large copper-coloured craft chain

4 x large jump rings

4 x headpins

Large copper-coloured lobster clasp

4 x felt balls

7 x sequins

Tools:

Cutting pliers

Round-nosed pliers

Instructions:

1 Open up the petals on the large bronze flower to reveal the central hole. Take a headpin and thread on to it a sequin and a felt ball.

2 Thread the headpin down through the centre of the flower and using round-nosed pliers, create a loop. Bend this slightly to one side so the flower will sit nicely.

3 Cut two lengths of chain, one shorter then the other. Attach both pieces to the large lobster clasp using a jump ring.

4 Open up the loop on the bronze flower once again, slip the bottom link of the longer chain through, then close once more.

5 Wire up the three remaining felt balls, remembering to add a sequin at each end. Add them to the chain wherever you wish.

Autumn Flower

This autumn-coloured alternative makes a really striking charm that is not
for the faint-hearted fashion lover! Bronze teamed with bright, warm colours
make a beautiful statement wherever the charm is displayed.

Disco Diva

Materials:

A selection of
   large sequins

Organza ribbon

Large silver-coloured
   lobster clasp

2 x feature beads

Tools:

Scissors

Instructions:

1 Thread the organza ribbon through the fixing point of the lobster clasp. Hold the two lengths of ribbon together and make a single knot just underneath the fixing point to secure.

2 Thread the sequins on one by one and tie each one on to the ribbon using a single knot, remembering to leave a gap between each sequin to allow the ribbon to show through.

3 Work both ribbon lengths in the same manner, finishing with a feature bead at the base to add decoration and a bit of weight to hold the ribbon in place.

Note: If your sequins or feature beads have small holes, you can use a collapsible eye needle to thread the ribbon through.

Razzle-Dazzle

Acid yellow and copper-coloured sequins adorn a peach-coloured ribbon, and the feature beads are a two-toned flower and a butterfly to complete this flighty but dazzling charm.

Egyptian Goddess

Materials:

2 x bronze triangle shapes

7 jump rings

6 headpins

Large copper-coloured lobster clasp

23 copper-coloured seed beads

A selection of 4mm and 6mm crystals

Suede ribbon

Flat leather crimp

Tools:

Cutting pliers

Round-nosed pliers

Instructions:

1 Take the two bronze shapes and join them, points together, using a jump ring.

2 For the bottom fringing, take five headpins and thread them with a mixture of crystals and seed beads, leaving enough spare wire at the top of each headpin to form a loop.

3 Re-open the loops and secure them through the fixing points on the triangle shape.

4 Decorate a sixth headpin and attach it to the jump ring that holds the two triangle shapes together.

5 Add a jump ring to each of the five fixing points at the other end of the piece.

6 Thread the suede ribbon through them, then place the two ends of suede ribbon into a flat leather crimp and secure them.

7 Finally, add the large lobster clasp by placing a jump ring through the fixing point of the flat leather crimp and closing it once the lobster clasp has been threaded on.

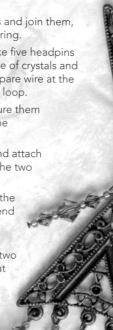

Fiery Fancy
Here a single triangle makes a simple but stunning charm, dripping with hot-coloured beads.

Victorian Elegance

Materials:

2 x heart shapes

Medium copper-coloured craft chain

6 x headpins

9 x jump rings

Large copper-coloured lobster clasp

A selection of large, medium and small faux
    pearl beads

Tools:

Cutting pliers

Round-nosed pliers

Instructions:

1 Cut two lengths of craft chain, one longer than the other, and using a
jump ring, attach them to the large lobster clasp.

2 Using headpins, wire up six sets of faux pearl beads.

3 Secure them to the fixing points at the base of each heart shape using
jump rings.

4 Attach the heart shapes to the ends of the chains using jump rings.

Heartfelt

This bronze and pearl charm is trimmed with 4mm fire-polished crystals as a glittering finishing touch.

Publisher's Note

If you would like more books on the techniques shown,
try the following:

80 Original Charms by Martine Routier, Search Press, 2007

Beading Basics by Stephanie Burnham,
Barron's Educational Series, 2006

The Encyclopedia of Beading Techniques by
Sara Withers & Stephanie Burnham, Search Press, 2005

Acknowledgements

Many thanks to The Bead Scene for supplying all the
beads and equipment used in this book.

The Bead Scene
PO Box 6351
Towcester
Northamptonshire
NN12 7YX

Website: www.thebeadscene.com
email: Stephanie@thebeadscene.com
Tel: 01327 353639